Greyhounds

Heather Kissock

www.openlightbox.com

Step 1
Go to **www.openlightbox.com**

Step 2
Enter this unique code
HAJNTSLO4

Step 3
Explore your interactive eBook!

AV2 is optimized for use on any device

Your interactive eBook comes with...

Contents
Browse a live contents page to easily navigate through resources

Audio
Listen to sections of the book read aloud

Videos
Watch informative video clips

Weblinks
Gain additional information for research

Slideshows
View images and captions

Try This!
Complete activities and hands-on experiments

Key Words
Study vocabulary, and complete a matching word activity

Quizzes
Test your knowledge

Share
Share titles within your Learning Management System (LMS) or Library Circulation System

Citation
Create bibliographical references following the Chicago Manual of Style

This title is part of our AV2 digital subscription

1-Year K–5 Subscription
ISBN 978-1-7911-3320-7

Access hundreds of AV2 titles with our digital subscription.
Sign up for a FREE trial at **www.openlightbox.com/trial**

Greyhounds

Contents

AV2 Book Code 2
Name That Dog 4
A Noble Dog.. 6
Fast and Sleek....................................11
A Gentle Soul.................................... 14
Greyhound Puppies 18
Greyhounds at Work....................... 23
Caring for a Greyhound................. 27
Greyhound Quiz...............................30
Key Words/Index 31

Name That Dog

Which dog can run at speeds up to 45 miles per hour?

What kind of dog was the mascot for a bus company?

What type of dog is mentioned in some versions of the Bible?

Which dog was a favorite of the Egyptian queen Cleopatra?

If you said the greyhound...

You are correct!

A Noble Dog

The greyhound is the world's oldest **purebred** dog. No one is sure where these dogs first appeared, but they may have originally been **bred** more than 8,000 years ago. Some believe that the **breed** was raised by European people known as the Celts. Others believe that the dogs are originally from the Middle East. However, greyhounds are most often associated with Egypt. Paintings of these dogs have been found on the walls of many ancient Egyptian buildings.

The Egyptians kept greyhounds as both companions and hunting dogs. The dogs were favorite pets of Egypt's rulers. King Tutankhamun and Queen Cleopatra both owned greyhounds.

Egypt is a country in northern Africa. It shares its borders with the countries of Libya, Sudan, and Israel, as well as a territory called the Gaza Strip.
Mediterranean Sea
Israel
Gaza Strip
Jordan
Saudi Arabia
Libya
Egypt
Red Sea
Sudan

Greyhounds continued to be the favorite dog of the upper classes for centuries. They were valued in many countries for their hunting skills and their noble appearance. In England, for many years, only the **nobility** could own greyhounds. They were the only group given royal permission to do so.

The American Kennel Club (AKC) recognized the greyhound as an official dog breed in 1885, one year after the organization was founded.

In the 1700s, people began to pay more attention to the speeds greyhounds could reach. By the 1900s, greyhound racing had become a popular event in England and other countries. People from all walks of life went to the races to bet on their favorite dog and hope for a win. Greyhound races are not as popular as they were in the past. They are now banned in many U.S. states.

Today, many greyhounds live their lives as family pets or **service** dogs. Their loyal, gentle nature makes them well-suited for both roles.

A greyhound's small waist gives the dog's body a distinct "S" shape.

Fast and Sleek

Greyhounds are large, sleek dogs. Adult males are 28 to 30 inches (71 to 76 centimeters) tall at the **withers**. They weigh between 65 and 70 pounds (29 and 32 kilograms). Full-grown females are only slightly shorter, and weigh anywhere from 5 to 10 pounds (2 to 5 kg) less.

A greyhound has a long head and neck. This dog's broad chest tapers to a tiny waist. A greyhound has very muscular hind legs. They provide the dog with the push it needs to sprint at speeds of up to 45 miles (72 kilometers) per hour. A greyhound's **streamlined** body carries almost no fat.

The greyhound breed is mentioned by name in some versions of the Christian Bible.

Some people believe the word "greyhound" comes from two Old English words. *Grei* means "dog" and *hundr* means "hunter."

Greyhounds have incredible eyesight. They belong to a hunting group called sighthounds. While some hunting dogs find **prey** using their noses, a greyhound uses its eyes. Greyhounds can see more than 0.5 miles (0.8 km) in front of them. Their eyes sit far apart on their narrow heads, giving them a 270-degree range of vision. This means that greyhounds do not have to turn their heads to see objects behind them. Their vision is **stereoscopic**, so they are able to see moving objects clearly. This helps greatly when tracking prey.

Many people think that greyhounds were named for their color. However, gray is actually just one of 18 greyhound coat colors. Others include black, white, tan, and **brindle**. A greyhound with a gray coat is said to be blue. No matter what color a greyhound is, it will have a short and smooth coat.

A running greyhound spends about 75 percent of its time in the air.

A Gentle Soul

Even though greyhounds have been bred to hunt and race, they are not **aggressive** dogs. They are quiet in nature. Greyhounds are considered to be a gentle dog breed.

Greyhounds prefer to avoid conflict. They rarely show anger. If someone or something annoys them, they will walk away. The only time greyhounds may get excited is when a small animal is around. Then, their hunting instincts might spring into action and they will go on the chase. It is best to keep small, active animals away from a greyhound.

Greyhounds generally get along well with other dogs. However, they should be supervised when around smaller dogs, especially ones they do not know.

A greyhound can sleep for up to 18 hours each day.

For the most part, greyhounds are "couch potatoes." They like to spread out on a sofa and sleep for much of the day. If there is room, and their owners want to join them, they welcome the company. Greyhounds love to spend time with their family, and enjoy both showing and receiving affection.

Greyhounds may get anxious if they are left alone for too long. They are very sensitive dogs. Their feelings can be hurt easily, and they may take a while to get over anything they see as an insult. Owners must make sure that their greyhound feels like it is part of the family.

Greyhounds may take a while to warm up to strangers. They will often stay close to their owners when meeting new people. They rarely bark, but may do so if someone is at the door.

Greyhound Puppies

A greyhound mother will usually have 1 to 12 puppies in a **litter**. The average litter size is eight puppies. Each greyhound puppy weighs between 0.3 and 1 pound (0.1 and 0.5 kg).

During their first few weeks, greyhound puppies rely on milk from their mothers for food. The puppies grow quickly. By the time they are one month old, they weigh between 2 and 5 pounds (0.9 and 2.3 kg). It is at this time that they can begin eating other types of food. Once they stop drinking their mothers' milk, they can leave their mothers and go to new homes.

Greyhound puppies cannot see or hear for their first two to three weeks.

Unlike adult greyhounds, puppies have high energy levels and are almost always on the move. They love to play, and will run around and wrestle with their siblings. As greyhound puppies grow bigger, it is important for owners to make sure that the dogs have space to run and stretch their legs.

A greyhound reaches its adult size between 13 and 14 months of age. It may take a little more time for its chest to fill out, however. A greyhound's calm personality begins to appear over time. By about three years of age, with proper training, a greyhound will have outgrown most of its puppy behaviors.

Instead of getting puppies, many people adopt retired racing greyhounds as pets. More than 280,000 have been adopted since the 1990s in the United States alone.

A greyhound's calm, gentle personality makes it an ideal breed for many different kinds of jobs.

Greyhounds at Work

Greyhound racing does not draw the crowds it once did. In many countries, people have grown concerned that racing the dogs is unfair to them and have banned greyhound races. Today, most greyhounds have found new jobs to perform instead.

Some greyhounds are now being trained as service dogs. These dogs help people in wheelchairs or with other mobility issues. Greyhounds have been trained to turn on lights, open doors, and retrieve dropped items. Greyhounds are large, stable dogs. They can provide support to someone who has trouble walking or going up and down stairs.

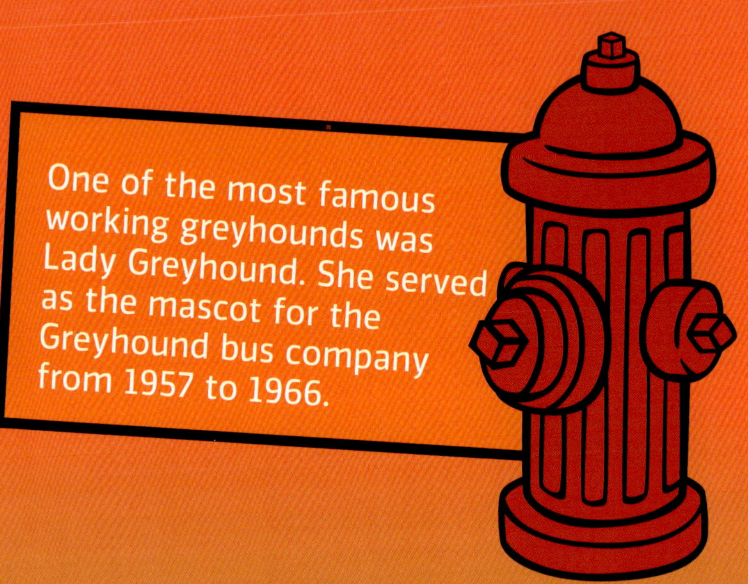

Some greyhounds help people with **post-traumatic stress disorder (PTSD)**. Loud noises may stress these people. Crowds may make them feel closed in. Being a sensitive dog, a greyhound can pick up on these emotions and help its owner to feel calm and safe. The dog might do this by leaning into someone's leg so that the person does not feel alone.

The greyhound's friendly, laid-back nature also makes it a good therapy dog breed. A therapy dog provides affection and comfort to a variety of people besides its owner. Some therapy greyhounds visit hospitals and seniors' homes. Others listen to children with learning challenges read stories. They support people in a way that helps people feel better about themselves.

At one time, Lady Greyhound's fan club had more than 500,000 members.

Training can help keep a greyhound under control. Greyhounds learn by praise, not punishment.

Caring for a Greyhound

In some ways, greyhounds are low-maintenance dogs. Their short hair requires little grooming. They are content with only a couple of walks per day. Still, these dogs have special areas that need the attention of a caring and observant owner.

Having a short coat means that greyhounds feel the cold more than other types of dogs. They cannot be left outside in cold weather for very long. When going for a winter walk, they should be dressed for the weather. A jacket will help keep a greyhound warm. Greyhounds should not spend too much time outside in the summer, either. Their short coats do not protect them from the heat.

A healthy greyhound can live up to 15 years. The average life span for this type of dog is 10 to 13 years.

Greyhounds can spring into action quickly, especially if they see something to chase. When walking in a public area, they should always be on a leash. If they are to be let out into a backyard, a high fence is a necessity. These will ensure that the dog does not get loose or run away.

Greyhounds are considered one of the healthiest dog breeds. However, they are prone to some health issues. These include stomach, eye, and heart problems. Regular visits to the **veterinarian** are important. Veterinarians are trained to tell when a dog is not feeling well and can take steps to improve its health.

Greyhounds can have poor dental health. Owners should brush their dog's teeth regularly with a special toothpaste.

Greyhound Quiz

Q: What kind of hunting dog is a greyhound?

A: A sighthound

Q: In what year did the AKC recognize the greyhound as an official dog breed?

A: 1885

Q: How many colors can greyhound coats be?

A: 18

Q: Which greyhound served as the mascot for the Greyhound bus company?

A: Lady Greyhound

Q: How many puppies can a greyhound mother have in one litter?

A: 1 to 12

Q: What is the average life span of a greyhound?

A: 10 to 13 years

Key Words

aggressive (uh-GREH-suhv): mean or unfriendly; likely to start a fight

bred (BRED): raised in a specific way

breed (BREED): a certain type of animal

brindle (BRIN-dl): a brownish color of animal fur, with streaks of other colors

litter (LI-tr): a group of babies born to one animal at the same time

nobility (no-BI-luh-tee): a class of people ranked immediately below royalty

post-traumatic stress disorder (PTSD) (POST truh-MAH-tuhk STRES dis-OR-dr): a health condition that can cause panic or terror in people who have experienced shocking events

prey (PRAY): an animal that is hunted by other animals

purebred (PYUR-bred): an animal with parents that are both the same breed

service (SUR-vuhs): working to help someone

stereoscopic (steh-ree-ow-SKAA-puhk): the ability to determine depth and distance by sight

streamlined (STREEM-lined): shaped for ease of movement

veterinarian (vehtr-uh-NEH-ree-uhn): a doctor who takes care of animals

withers (WI-thrz): the part of an animal that lies at the base of the neck, above the shoulders

Index

adoption 21
American Kennel Club (AKC) 8, 30

Bible 12

Celts 6
coat 12, 27, 30

Egypt 6, 7
England 8, 9
eyesight 12, 18

Greyhound bus company 24, 30

height 11
hunting 6, 8, 12, 14, 30

King Tutankhamun 6

Lady Greyhound 24, 25, 30
life span 28, 30

puppies 18, 19, 20, 21, 30

Queen Cleopatra 6

service dogs 9, 23

therapy 24
training 20, 23, 26, 28

veterinarian 28

weight 11, 18

Get the best of both worlds.

AV2 bridges the gap between print and digital.

The expandable resources toolbar enables quick access to content including **videos**, **audio**, **activities**, **weblinks**, **slideshows**, **quizzes**, and **key words**.

Animated videos make static images come alive.

Resource icons on each page help readers to further **explore key concepts**.

Published by Lightbox Learning Inc.
276 5th Avenue, Suite 704 #917
New York, NY 10001
Website: www.openlightbox.com

Library of Congress Control Number: 2022933070

ISBN 978-1-7911-4799-0 (hardcover)
ISBN 978-1-7911-4800-3 (softcover)
ISBN 978-1-7911-4326-8 (multi-user eBook)

Printed in Guangzhou, China
1 2 3 4 5 6 7 8 9 0 26 25 24 23 22

022022
101321

Project Coordinator: John Willis
Designer: Terry Paulhus

Photo Credits
Every reasonable effort has been made to trace ownership and to obtain permission to reprint copyright material. The publisher would be pleased to have any errors or omissions brought to its attention so that they may be corrected in subsequent printings. The publisher acknowledges Alamy, Minden Pictures, Getty Images, and Shutterstock as its primary image suppliers for this title.